SELF WISE

By Caroline Towers

Self Wise
By Caroline Towers

ISBN: 978-1-7391000-0-1

Published by: Caroline Towers
Copyeditor and proofreader: Siân-Elin Flint-Freel
Book design by: Michelle Catanach

All information, methods, techniques and advice contained within this publication reflect the views and experiences of the author, whose intent is to provide readers with various choices and options. We are all individuals with different beliefs and viewpoints, therefore it is recommended that readers carry out their own research prior to making any such choices. While all attempts have been made to verify the information contained within this book, neither the author nor the publisher assume responsibility for any errors or omissions, or for any actions taken or results experienced by any reader.

To all the spirited women who dare to dream and strive for a life they adore – this is for you. You're not just deserving of joy and success; you're capable of creating it.

CONTENTS

"I was born wise. Street-wise, people-wise, self-wise. This wisdom was my birthright."

Sophia Loren

CHAPTER 1

HOW TO BE SELF WISE

Where are you now?

Are you feeling unfulfilled with your current career path or business venture? Have you been searching for something that brings you joy and a sense of purpose? If so, you are not alone. Many women find themselves in a job or business that they are not passionate about but feel stuck because it pays the bills.

However, life is too short to spend most your time doing something that doesn't bring you happiness.

If you believe that you need to do what you love to be truly satisfied and fulfilled in your work, then Self Wise is for you. Whether you are just starting out or have been in business for a while, Self Wise will provide you with insights and strategies to grow a business doing what you love. How good is that?!

Starting a business is now easier than ever before. You can start one or more businesses with just a few clicks online. However, many people who want to start a business think it's the starting which is the hard part – and sometimes it can be if you procrastinate. It might feel difficult and complicated to decide what you want to do, but once you have made the decision you can dive straight in. Actually, starting can be the easiest part.

But here's the catch: succeeding and keeping your business afloat can at times bring challenges. Self Wise will take you through the process of deciding on a business that works for you. If you choose a business which suits you, then it is so much easier to be successful.

Self-belief

So if it's not the starting which is tough, what is?

It's the success, the keeping going, the self-doubt, the not knowing what to do and so much more. All of these things can make you procrastinate, and worse than that, stop you in your tracks. You might go searching for the next online course or another online teacher's words of advice, jumping from one to the other to get 'the answer'.

I don't want you to do this, or if you have been doing this (like I did for many years), I want you to stop right now.

Building a business which is fulfilling and brings you joy doesn't have to be difficult. In fact, you probably already know much more than you realise. You know all about the product or service that you are creating, you probably know plenty about the industry your business is in and you already have the desire within yourself – that's a good starting point.

Having the want to start and build a business, combined with understanding yourself and knowing some of the business basics, will help you overcome any beliefs you have that you can't do it or that it's not going to work for you.

Based on my experience of working with women in business for the past twenty years, the most common fear I have seen is all about self-belief.

Once you believe in yourself, you can be unstoppable in creating your business. When you know what makes you work at your best, when you understand the principles of business and know how to keep yourself going when you have some doubts, then there will be no stopping you!

The answer is within you

Self Wise is all about you and your business. What sort of person are you? What drives you? Who can help you? What do you want to achieve? What is your 'why'?

There was/is a good reason you wanted to start your own business. Perhaps it was to make more money, to live a life with freedom and flexibility, or maybe it was to do something which made you happy. It might even be a little piece of all of these. Whatever it is, you have to make a start.

But there is so much information out there online. Often, if you Google one thing you will get hundreds of different answers. When you do this for your business, you then feel overwhelmed, can procrastinate, and start to see yourself as failing.

The one thing I never want you to see yourself as is a failure.

Starting a business is brave and it's not for everyone. If you're searching for answers to bring yourself more success, then it shows you have the desire within you and that you are more than capable. It's time for you to search within, instead of always looking to others. To learn how you can use your skills – and ultimately your own wisdom – to build the success you are craving right now.

Me, I have built multiple businesses and I've not always done it well. I've wasted valuable time and money always searching for an easier way or a better way to achieve my goals. Until one day, I realised that I did know what I was doing. Yes, sometimes I can look to teachers for help when I see a gap in my understanding, but I found I was often learning about the same topics from different people over and over again. I had the facts and the information within me but what was missing was the understanding about myself, how I like to work and what skills I was bringing to the business table.

I want to help you avoid some of the common mistakes that new business owners make. I want you to get clarity and focus much faster than I did because I believe that when women build wonderful businesses, then the world can be a much better place.

With hard work and dedication, you can learn a lot and progress quickly.

Keeping going

One of the things I love is seeing women set themselves up in business. Many years ago, I used to go to a lot of networking events and would often speak to women who were new in business. I loved it and often felt like a seasoned veteran, even if I was only a few years ahead.

Sadly, some of those women didn't come back to the networking events after six months or so. I always hoped it was because their businesses had taken off so much that they no longer had the time. Although I am sure that is true for some, I am positive that for others it's because they closed their business. Stopping their businesses could have been for all sorts of reasons: they couldn't make the income they needed, weren't able to balance their family and business life, found it was too much pressure, discovered they didn't actually like running a business of their own, or something else.

I don't want this for you. I want you to keep going, to understand how you can use your skills and your personality to build something right for you with the lifestyle you crave. I want you to build the life that you want. By lifestyle, I mean creating a business that aligns with your values and allows you to achieve your personal and professional aims.

Building a successful business for you

What is success? We will come to that big question later. It's important to define success on your own terms and build a business that aligns with your unique vision and goals.

Don't be swayed too much by what others have done, be it friends, people in the public eye or even family. What is success for them may not be what is right for you. That's not to say that you can't learn from them. However, you might not have many – or even any – people in your life who have built a successful business. In which case, you have nobody else to learn from in your personal life. But that doesn't mean that you can't be successful.

In Self Wise, I'll share my experience and insights to help you build a successful business that aligns with your goals and values. I was lucky, my mum and stepdad had their own business so I had some experience of the business world from a young age and also people to talk to when things got tough or I felt stuck, but it still took time. That's why I felt compelled to write Self Wise, to help you reach your success more quickly than I ever did. To be your friend in your back pocket who can give you some guidance, shares some highs and some lows as well as everything in between. To help you understand yourself better and ultimately encourage you to believe in yourself more.

It's usual to have doubts and worries, and to be honest, I didn't realise that at first. I thought once you started, you had to be positive all of the time to attract sales or clients. If you felt an ounce of negativity, then that would be it, your life and business would be over. What I want to share with you is how you can overcome some of the doubts that you might have in yourself. I am here to be your biggest cheerleader, because if you ever spend any time with me, you know that I will also encourage you to go after your dreams, build the business and build up your confidence. What you learn in Self Wise will give you a chance to believe in yourself, know what you want to do within the business and do it with confidence and clarity.

I don't subscribe to working all of the time either. There was a time when I felt like I always needed to be in front of a screen.

I'll be honest with you – I might have been sat in front of a computer but I wasn't always doing anything useful. I was usually procrastinating more than working. I used to think I had to be glued to my laptop day and night to be successful. This couldn't be further from the truth. Just a few days ago I had one of my best sales days in quite a while when I was out having fun, drinking champagne in the VIP area of a cycle race!

When you build a business, work becomes a big part of your life. It's up to you to find the right blend, but I want you to know from the beginning of this book that your business doesn't have to be everything. It can be a huge part of your life, but you must make room for other people and things too. A lesson I've had to learn the hard way at times.

It's not always easy to know when to stop working when you enjoy your business and you want to achieve specific things each day, week, month or year. I know I can still have trouble turning off both my brain and my laptop at times, but when I do, I always come back better and refreshed.

Once I understood how I can work at my best, what things in life bring me joy and what works for my life, then I began working better, doing less and still achieved more success.

You deserve to be happy

I strongly believe that having joy in your life is crucial. Although it may seem obvious, many people (including myself) have gone through periods of life without much fun. However, you (just like me) are worthy of having some fun every day. You don't have to quit your job and travel the world, but adding elements of happiness to your daily routine can make a big difference. Life is short, so why not give yourself the happiness you deserve?

If your initial reaction is that you don't deserve happiness, or that you certainly don't deserve it every day, please stick with

> *Do something in the next twenty-four hours that brings a smile to your face.*

me. There is a large portion of society who believes that misery is something to be worn like a badge of honour, but it's time to change that. Stop throwing pity parties and feeling sorry for yourself. Instead, grab life with both hands and do something in the next twenty-four hours that brings a smile to your face, no matter how simple or frivolous it may seem. Moving into a state of happiness, even if only for a moment, can change everything in your day.

How it all began

Let me take you back to the early 2000s, just after I finished school. For the most part, school was a positive experience for me. I was lucky to have some wonderful friends and a few good teachers, and I enjoyed learning. I always said that I never wanted to work in an office and wanted to work for myself, but I had no idea how to do that, and even if I had, I had no capital or ideas to make it work. So, I set out to get myself a job.

My first 'real' job was for a third-party mortgage company. I started in the lowest department, managing the deeds to properties, and quickly realised that my skills weren't always going to be valued. Even though I knew this, I got comfortable, made some friends, and enjoyed my time in a low-paid job. I was easily meant for more, but when I asked for a pay rise during my review, I was told no, even though I was doing more tasks than the role demanded, such as standing in for my manager when they were away. This taught me that no matter how much you value yourself, there is often too much office politics going on for others to value you. I started to doubt the quality of my work and my commitment, despite doing a side project with one of the company's big wigs who even knew my name and thought I was wonderful. I stayed in this job for much longer than I should have, even though I was always on a temporary contract. (This was my choice because deep down there was a part of me that knew this wasn't where I wanted to be forever.)

My next role was the first time I took on a permanent position, which lasted only six months. I was offered a job in the repossessions department, and I accepted it because it paid more and gave me a chance to show my skills. I worked in a call centre, taking call after call from people in one of the worst moments of their lives, losing their homes. It was incredibly depressing to tell people to pay up or get out. I had to pass on what the client offered to pay to a senior mortgage person to see if it would be accepted, and then let them know if they and their families could spend another few nights with a roof over their heads. It was quickly time to move on, but I was stuck in this nine to five job because I needed to pay for my car, and like many people in their early twenties, my much loved nights out. Like most people, I needed money to live.

I knew that I didn't want to have a permanent role, so I went back to my initial job agency, and they placed me in a social services department. Like many of these organisations, there were some wonderful people who worked there, full of skills and enthusiasm, but over time, it gets beaten out of them, mainly by bad bosses.

One boss, Chris, used to have a strop and shout at our little team of three in front of everyone. Who can work and respect a grown man who behaves like this? Certainly not me! It's amazing what you will put up with at work.

When it was finally time to leave, I don't remember Chris even saying goodbye, but I do remember the rest of the building giving me a great send-off! I was only moving next door, but in social services terms, it was miles away!

In the next job, I was the person you would speak to if you had a concern about a child. It was another not-so-cheery role of talking to families in the worst moments of their life. It felt like a running theme for me; I kept having the jobs with the most depressing of subjects.

Again, the people made the job good and this time I had a lovely boss too. I stayed for much longer than I should have done but by this time I had bought a house with my boyfriend and so now had more financial commitments. I had finally done it, got stuck in a cycle of working, sleeping and come Sunday evening, dreading work. Now it felt like there was no way out.

I was so fortunate that I was able to stay temporary, even when my manager asked me to go permanent. I think it would have saved them some money but I resisted. It was my one chance at having some kind of freedom in my life – I just didn't realise it.

Oh, and yes, my boyfriend and I were able to get a mortgage, both on temporary job contracts (he had just changed jobs when we bought a house). Hello, the housing boom of 2008 – or should I say crash, which happened about a month later!

I have always liked nice things, going out with friends and living the good life. I also am not averse to working hard but somewhere along the way, I felt like I was doing the work without living the fun life. When Sundays would roll around far too quickly, I would dread the next day coming. Work wasn't 'bad' but I felt like that there was no joy. Friday nights and

Saturdays were recovering from a week of work and Sundays were a day of worrying about a week of work. It was a vicious cycle.

Eventually, I reached a tipping point. Maybe you can relate? I needed to do more, do something else and do something for myself. So I applied and was accepted at my local university to study creative writing and English literature. I didn't think about it too much; I was desperate to do something else. I had twice been accepted to study English at university previously and then backed out before going into the workforce, so it was something I had a pull towards.

It was the best thing I ever did. Not because of what I learnt – although I did enjoy almost every moment of learning something new – but more because of what that leap led me to.

I was so fortunate that for the first year, my manager let me work part-time. My colleague had a sister who was looking for some part-time admin work at her charity and so I also did that in my own time. This was the first time I experienced what it was like to work for myself.

I also started to help more in the family business again, now social media was taking off. I could use this to practise and learn more about the online world.

With these different roles and a supportive boyfriend, I could support myself through university. I thought if I did something for three years which brought me joy in my whole working life, then that would be enough.

It wasn't.

Once I graduated, I didn't want to give up the joy of working for myself. I continued to work as a freelancer and also helped other businesses with their social media. My mum would often drag me to business networking events, and although I didn't always want to go as the introvert in me found them hard, they helped me build my own business.

I started a health and wellness product-based business in the network marketing industry, which I did for a few years. So, with this and my freelance work, I was able to avoid going back to work in an office.

All of this opened my eyes to a new way of working, which was so much fun. I also started dabbling with my own blog around this time. I would take courses and then implement them into my blog, as well as implementing anything I learned into the family business and with any clients I had.

Going to university had opened up this new way of working and learning, and I couldn't get enough of it. Each day was exciting as I learned more, implemented what I was learning, and made some money doing it. Finally, I felt like I could have both joy and an income without sacrificing one for the other.

This was the way I worked for a few years. And it suited me.

There were many things I enjoyed about the network marketing industry, but one of the best was learning about mindset, which I will talk more about later. Having this understanding helped me create a more positive mindset, something I continue to work on today. Trust me, this is always an ongoing process!

After a few years, though, I felt a little bit stuck, which is normal for any business. I loved my blog and my clients, but I didn't always like working for them. It felt like a job instead of running my own business. So I created an online course and coaching business to teach others about blogging and content creation, and eventually sold that business.

I've certainly pivoted and picked up new projects and businesses along the way. It's been a wild ride (and still is!), and even on the bad days, there is always some good.

All the years of learning and pivoting have led me to this place where I am right now.

As I am writing this, I do very little client work apart from a few whom I have worked with for years. Instead, I have built a number of e-commerce businesses.

I love creating new products and designs and marketing them.

15

I also love to write still so I have focused a lot on being creative and encouraging others to find their own creativity. This is what I know I am good at, and finally, all the years of learning and pivoting have led me to this place where I am right now.

N N N

This book is a place of compassion, joy, and happiness. Learning how to be happy in your life – including your work life. Not every day will be the best day of your life, but each day can have good moments in it.

As I've said, I love to see women setting themselves up in business. There are so many opportunities in today's world to build the business and life of your dreams. Yes, it takes work, but it's possible to do it.

I believe with every cell of my body that you can create the success you desire as a female in business. Once you know what business you want to achieve, how you keep growing, what support you might need, and have the self-belief and wisdom, then you can achieve!

"Do not be afraid to be yourself. That's when you're going to be your happiest."

Stevie Nicks

CHAPTER 2
UNDERSTANDING YOURSELF AND HOW YOU WORK

Have you ever taken a moment to reflect on what truly brings you joy in life? It's not just about what you enjoy doing in your work, but which activities, hobbies or experiences light you up and make you feel fulfilled. This chapter is all about discovering those things and incorporating more of them into your daily life. So, take a moment to think about what makes you happy and let's dive into how you can incorporate more of it into your life.

Starting your own business is a journey that not only teaches you about the business world but also about yourself. It requires you to step out of your comfort zone, learn new skills, and put yourself out there to let the world know about your business. It can be an exciting and rewarding experience, but it can also be daunting and challenging. In this chapter, we will also explore how understanding yourself and your business can help you navigate the ups and downs of entrepreneurship.

The Entrepreneurial Rollercoaster

Starting a business can be an emotional rollercoaster. You will experience highs and lows, moments of self-doubt, and moments of pure joy. It's essential to understand that this is all part of the journey, and it's normal to have a multitude of emotions every day. As a business owner, you are responsible for everything, from the success of your business to the well-being of your employees. It can be overwhelming, but it's important to know that you are not alone. Many entrepreneurs face the same challenges and emotions.

Knowing Yourself

As a woman in business, you may have different roles and responsibilities in your personal life to those in your business. You may have a family, care for a relative, have a busy social life, or many hobbies and interests you want to pursue. You may also find that your personality can be different when you are in business mode compared to when you are at home. Understanding your strengths, weaknesses, and tendencies in both your personal and professional life can help you make the most of your skills and abilities.

It's also okay to recognise that you may not be perfect at everything in your business. Making mistakes is part of the learning process, and it's essential to keep learning about the business world and yourself. Once you start to learn about yourself and what motivates you, you can use that knowledge to focus your energy on the areas where you excel.

Aligning Yourself with Your Business

Starting your own business is a journey that teaches you about the business world and yourself. Understanding your strengths, weaknesses, and tendencies can help you navigate the ups and downs of entrepreneurship. Remember that learning about yourself is an ongoing process, and you are always evolving as a human being and as a businesswoman so never stop.

As an entrepreneur, it's easy to fall into the trap of trying to do everything and please everyone. However, it's essential to recognise the times when you're trying to do something that doesn't align with your personality or values. For example, if you're not a numbers person, creating a business based around finance may not be the best fit for you.

Recognising your strengths and bringing them into your business can help you succeed and goes a long way to help you enjoy your work.

There have been times in the past when I've realised that I was trying to do something that didn't align with my personality.

I was attempting to do something that wasn't my forté. For instance, I once took a course and then spent a few months selling insurance. As someone who is not a numbers person, this didn't bring me any joy at all – and to be honest, it didn't make me much money either! But now I know that being creative and working for myself is how I work best and suits my personality – so that's what I do!

I discovered this by taking a personality test, which can be an excellent tool for getting to know yourself better and understand what makes you tick. I know it might seem like a way to procrastinate and you may be sceptical about what you can learn about yourself from an online test. But a business coach of mine recommended it, and I trusted her advice. The test I took is the Myers-Briggs personality test, which is available at 16personalities.com.

The 16 Personalities test provides you with a complete breakdown of your personality and how you can apply it to all aspects of your life. My first encounter with Myers-Briggs was at a business training event with my mum, who also has her own business. We took the test, and our results were so different. My mum is an extrovert, whereas I am an introvert, and we were nearly opposites on all parts of the test results.

This explained so much. Often, when my mum would suggest something, I would cringe at the thought, particularly when it came to speaking to people, which she could do effortlessly. It just goes to show that even a mother and daughter can be so different, but can still build businesses – they just each do it in their own way.

Apart from knowing that I had a different approach to business to my mum, I didn't think much about Myers-Briggs after the event until years later my coach recommended that I retake the test. I couldn't recall my personality type, so I thought it was a good idea.

When I saw the results on 16 Personalities, it was a revelation. It was as if someone had reached into my brain and was describing me. I couldn't believe it. I was part of a small business coaching group and the coach recommended we take the test. All the women at the time said the same thing. Even though we all had different results, we finally felt heard!

If you're curious, my personality type is INFP-T, also known as a Mediator.

Here is a snippet of what the opening of my description is:

"Although they may seem quiet or unassuming, Mediators (INFPs) have vibrant, passionate inner lives. Creative and imaginative, they happily lose themselves in daydreams, inventing all sorts of stories and conversations in their minds. Idealistic and empathetic, Mediators long for deep, soulful relationships, and they feel called to help others. But because this personality type makes up such a small portion of the population, Mediators may sometimes feel lonely or invisible, adrift in a world that doesn't seem to appreciate the traits that make them unique." *16personalities.com*

Woah, this was just the tip of the iceberg, but it felt so much like me. I won't copy and paste my whole personality because I am, after all, here to help you.

As the website suggests, there are 16 different personality types on the Myers-Briggs test. These are all different combinations, depending on how you answer the questions.

Each Myers-Briggs type has a unique four-letter code to identify them.

ISTJ – INSPECTOR: Reserved and practical, they are usually loyal, traditional and orderly.

ISTP – CRAFTER: They love new experiences, are independent and provide first-hand learning.

ISFJ – PROTECTOR: Warm-hearted and dedicated, they protect the people they care about.

ISFP – ARTIST: Artistic, reserved, flexible and easy-going.

INFJ – ADVOCATE: Creative and analytical.

INFP – MEDIATOR: Creative with high values, they want to make the world a better place.

INTJ – ARCHITECT: Creative, analytical and logical.

INTP – THINKER: Quiet and introverted, they like to have a rich inner world.

ESTP – PERSUADER: Dramatic, out-going and love to spend time with others whilst focusing on the here and now.

ESTJ – DIRECTOR: Assertive and follows the rules, they like to take charge and have high principles.

ESTP – PERFORMER: Spontaneous and outgoing they enjoy centre stage.

ESFJ – CAREGIVER: Outgoing and soft-hearted, they believe the best in others.

ENFP – CHAMPION: Energetic and charismatic, they like to put their creativity to work.

ENFJ – GIVER: Sensitive and loyal, they are usually generous and understanding.

ENTP – DEBATER: Inventive and although they love to start many projects they can struggle to finish them.

ENTJ – COMMANDER: Confident and outspoken, the like to be organised and make plans.

Having read the list, which do you think you might be?

Now I want you to put this book down for a moment and head to 16personalities.com to find out. Even if you have taken something similar in the past, you will benefit from doing it again.

Which personality type are you?

What are your personality traits?

How did you find the personality test? It can be scary when something is accurate about you!

Having a deeper understanding of yourself can truly transform your life. It can guide you towards your strengths, highlight areas where you may need help, and most importantly, help you accept and appreciate the fundamentals of who you are.

For me, knowing my personality type has helped me understand why I often feel drained after networking with my extroverted mum. While my mum can talk and socialise for hours, I usually hit a wall after just an hour or two. But there's nothing wrong with either of our approaches to networking, it's simply who we are. By accepting this fact, we've learned to work with each other's strengths and limitations.

If you work with team members or have family members who you regularly interact with, it can be helpful to encourage them to take a personality test too. This way, you can better understand how they feel and therefore work together more effectively.

For me, the test recommended pursuing a career as a writer and writing a book, which is exactly what I'm doing now. But that doesn't mean writing has always been the only thing I've done for the last twelve years of growing my business or the twenty years of my working life. However, writing has always been a key component, from blogging to writing captions on social media. When I think about it, I realise I've written almost every day. Writing and being creative is what really fires me up.

Your personality type is a great guideline. It's important to remember that they are not hard and fast rules, but rather a useful tool to refer back to when you feel stuck. They can guide you towards areas where you need help, and areas where you can work on improving.

For me, verbal communication is something I always have to work on. I find it hard to share my feelings and ask for help. By rereading my personality profile as I write this book, I've realised that there are still plenty of areas where I can improve, and verbal communication is one of them. That's the thing about business and finding yourself, as I've said before, it's an ongoing, never-ending process.

But the great thing about knowing your personality type is that you can use it as a foundation to build on, and continue to grow and learn about yourself.

Find joy in your life

Now that you have seen the accuracy of your test results, let's talk about something that is equally important: joy. Building a business and making money should be joyful. Perhaps you left your previous career because it was making you unhappy. Now that you are running the show, it is important to find things that bring you happiness.

Of course, not every task will be joyful. For instance, I don't enjoy inputting receipts for my accounts, but on that day, I also do things that bring me happiness. You must remember that you started your business to find fulfilment, freedom and satisfaction in your life. Maybe you are even pursuing your life's passion. That should be enjoyable! Creating products and services, making money, coming up with new ideas, and growing a business are all fantastic things you are doing right now.

Throughout this book, I urge you to keep trying to find things that bring you joy. After all, one of my mentors, Gala Darling, taught me that "the more fun I have, the more money I make."

The more fun I have, the more money I make.

Isn't that a great mantra to live by!

Once you find what you enjoy in business, you can have more fun every day. You can strike a balance between what brings you joy, what you know how to do, and how you can incorporate it into your life.

What are you good at?

Start by examining your experience. This could be in the business you have started or in any of your previous jobs. I have no doubt that you have many experiences that you could use to your advantage in your business.

Consider not only your experience but also what you are good at. When I first started working freelance, for instance, I was good at typing and English, so I worked briefly for a charity typing meeting notes. It was a way to use my skills in the short term while moving toward my bigger business goals.

I am confident that there are many things you are good at. When you combine these with your experience, personality type, and things that bring you joy, you can build the business of your dreams.

One of my clients, Mary, was amazing. She wanted to create a non-profit teenage brand and was also a personal assistant in her full-time job. She used her PA skills to create a virtual assistant agency because she already had those skills. It made sense for her to take what she was good at, what she enjoyed, and what she had experience in to generate an income for herself and ultimately fund her non-profit!

Keep doing what works for you

If you are already on your business journey, keep in mind what has worked for you so far. In my experience, it is easy to move on to the next bright, shiny thing – which I have done far too many times to count – but when I look back, there were things that were working in my business that I stopped doing.

For example, when I used to teach blogging online, being consistent on social media helped attract new clients and students. For some reason, I stopped being consistent, and the sign-ups stopped too. I only realised this later. Instead of doing the things that were working, I saw another shiny object and jumped right into it. It is essential to keep checking what is working, even if it can be difficult for creative, non-data-driven people like me.

Learn from my mistakes and keep checking what works in your business!

Learn from my mistakes and keep checking what works in your business!

When do you work best?

Lastly, understand the times of day (or night!) you work best. Traditionally, I was a night owl and always worked into the evening. However, over time, I have come to understand myself better and use my own wisdom to challenge this belief. I was only a night owl because I woke up late, wasn't organised, and had to rush to finish things. I convinced myself that this was how I was supposed to work.

After struggling with a lack of productivity, I decided to try something different. I started waking up earlier, thanks to my then boyfriend's job that required him to get up early. It wasn't an immediate change, but eventually I stopped hitting snooze and discovered that I was most productive and creative in the mornings. I found that I had more energy and enthusiasm for the day ahead and that my inbox wasn't inundated with emails when I opened my laptop!

Nowadays, I try to wake up early most days (even though I still don't love it), and by mid-late morning, I'll take a break to work out, go out for lunch, or just relax. Then, in the afternoon, after a brief post-lunch slump, I find that my energy returns and I can get some more work done before putting the computer away for the evening.

Of course, everyone has their own unique rhythm, and I'm not saying that being a night owl won't work for some people. But I encourage you to experiment with different working hours and find what works best for you. You might be surprised, as I was, by the results you get. And remember that your preferences may change over time as your life circumstances and responsibilities shift.

Nowadays, I try to avoid working in the evenings unless I have a burst of inspiration. I feel fortunate to be able to work at the times that suit me best, and that's one of the real freedoms of running your own business!

So, if you're struggling to find your optimal working hours, I encourage you to test different times of day and see what brings you joy and maximises your productivity. And don't forget to keep incorporating the activities and tasks that you enjoy into your day-to-day work routine. By combining your unique personality with what has worked for you in the past, you'll be well on your way to building a successful business that brings you fulfilment and joy.

✏ ✏ ✏

What to focus on:

✏ **Prioritise Joy in Business:** Remember that one of the reasons you started your own business was to find joy, fulfilment and freedom. Integrate tasks that bring you happiness alongside those that are mandatory but less enjoyable.

✗ **Leverage Your Skills and Experience:** Consider what you are good at and have experience in, then incorporate these into your business. For example, if you were a great typist in a past job, find a way to utilise that skill in your current venture.

✗ **Consistently Evaluate What Works:** Avoid being distracted by new opportunities at the expense of proven strategies. Stick with what has been effective in growing your business and consistently evaluate and adapt.

✗ **Identify Your Productive Times:** Experiment with working at different times of the day to find when you're most productive and joyful. Your optimal working hours can evolve, so be open to change.

✗ **Blend Joy and Productivity:** Continuously find a balance between what you enjoy, what you're skilled at, and what works in your business. This fusion will help sustain both your happiness and business success.

"I am not afraid. I was born to do this."

Joan of Arc

CHAPTER 3
KNOWING YOUR BUSINESS OPTIONS

In today's world, the range of business options available to us is truly amazing. It's always inspiring to see the variety of career paths people have taken, from photographers to solicitors to marketers and yoga teachers. It's my hope that children growing up today are aware of the vast array of possibilities open to them.

Unlike our parents or grandparents, who often stayed in one career for life, today's entrepreneurs have the freedom to explore multiple paths. This may be both exciting and overwhelming, as it can be difficult to determine which direction to take.

If you're reading this book, you may already have a business in mind. However, if things aren't going as planned, don't worry. I'm here to help you build a successful business, and that may require changing direction or trying something new.

There are several types of businesses you can build, including service-based businesses (e.g. social media management) and product-based businesses (e.g. selling handmade items). When choosing the right business for you, it's important to consider your personality type (as we discussed in the previous chapter). By building a business that aligns with your strengths and interests, you'll be more likely to find success and fulfilment.

> *If you're finding that every day is a challenge, take some time to reflect on what needs to change.*

Building a business takes hard work, but it shouldn't feel like a constant struggle. If you're finding that every day is a challenge, take some time to reflect on what needs to change.

One of the benefits of entrepreneurship is the ability to work from home. Whether you're working alone or building a team, a home-based business can provide the flexibility and autonomy that many entrepreneurs crave. Of course, it's not for everyone, so weigh up the pros and cons carefully.

If you're starting out on your own, it's okay to be a solopreneur and outsource work as needed. As you grow, you may decide to build a team, but that's a topic for a later chapter.

Ultimately, the businesses I'll be discussing in this book have infinite potential. Whether you're seeking financial success, flexibility, or something else entirely, your business can provide a path to achieving your goals.

Success means different things to different people, so it's important to define what a 'successful life' looks like for you. For many entrepreneurs, this means having the flexibility and freedom to pursue other interests, whether that's spending time with family or taking a mid-day yoga class. For others, it is financial freedom.

There are many different types of businesses available, and it's important to choose one that aligns with your strengths, circumstances and personality.

Types of business

As I say, there are loads of business ideas to choose from, but most of them fall into these categories. Have a read and see which one(s) appeal to you.

Service Business

When I first started in business, I began with a service-based business model. This involves offering your skills in exchange for payment. For my first self-employed role, I carried out admin work for a local charity. I would collect the work from them, complete it at home, and return it a week later when I picked up the next week's work. Utilising skills I had gained from years of office work allowed me to make some money while also offering flexibility in my work schedule. This allowed me to work during evenings and weekends, rather than the traditional 9-5. It was eye-opening to realise that I could get paid for working when I wanted and for a job that was easy for me.

This was just the beginning of my business journey, and I then moved into social media management. This was a skill I had learned for myself and my mum's bike shop. At the time, not many people knew how to set up a Facebook page, so I started there and grew a business with multiple long-term clients across different social media platforms like Instagram and Facebook. Again, this was a service-based business.

Service businesses offer a vast array of skills, from your more traditional businesses such as accountants and electricians to creatives like photography and social media. I believe that almost everyone could set up some kind of service business where they offer their skills and trade in exchange for payment.

Having a service business can be a great way to support your other passions. For example, my friend Jenny started a business as a photographer because she loved being creative and taking photos. However, she found that building a client base for wedding photography was taking time, so she also started personal training as this was something she had done in the past while working in a gym. This helped her supplement her income. Although it was challenging at times to build up both businesses, because she was experienced in personal training, she built up a regular client base. Once her wedding photography business started to grow, she could scale back the personal training.

This is a great example of using the skills you already have to support what you want to do.

When it comes to service businesses, you can often run them from anywhere. If you are looking for a lifestyle business, one that fits in with your life, then a service business is definitely something to consider. As well as being able to work from anywhere, they can be very scalable businesses (meaning there is a potential to grow). When I was a social media manager, I had considered building a team of other managers and turning the business into an agency. However, I decided this wasn't for me as I had other interests and businesses that I was more eager to grow. But it shows that you can take a solo business and grow it into something larger.

Like anything in life, there are pros and cons to running a service business. Here is a selection of them that might help you decide if it's right for you.

Here are some of the pros and cons of starting a service business:

Pros:

- ✗ Can usually work from anywhere.

- ✗ Only need a laptop and Wi-Fi.

- ✗ Can be very scalable.

- ✗ Can use the skills you already have.

- ✗ Have clients on a long-term retainer.

- ✗ Can set your prices.

- ✗ Have a global client base.

Cons:

- ✗ You have to find clients.

- ✗ Clients can contact you when you are not working.

- ✗ Clients can stop working with you.

- ✗ The work can be time-consuming.

- ✗ You may have to do work that is not your passion.

- ✗ Need to keep marketing your business while working on someone else's business.

- ✗ It is often an exchange of your time for money.

Product Business

A product business involves selling physical products to consumers, either through a physical shop or an e-commerce online store. You may choose to operate both a brick-and-mortar shop and an online store, or just one of them. Products can be created by you, sold from another company, or a combination of both.

There is a lot of potential in a product business, but it comes with significant financial investment in stock, premises, and other associated costs. You may also be tied to a physical shop, as it requires opening hours, and without staff, you need to be present throughout these hours.

However, with e-commerce, you can sell products online without worrying about a physical shop. You can utilise your marketing skills to create and sell products online. Unless you are making, storing, and shipping products yourself, you will need help with production, storage, or distribution. Starting a product business may seem overwhelming, but as you grow, you can outsource or build a team to manage these processes.

When starting an e-commerce business, it's important to consider the type of products you want to sell. If you don't want to create products yourself, print on demand can be a great option. With print on demand, you outsource the product production to a printer who can print and ship orders for you.

This model can be very efficient, flexible, and allows you to build a business from anywhere.

One of the benefits of a product business is that you can sell products all the time, even if you're not physically present. You have the potential to create a product and sell it globally to a large consumer market. However, you must invest hours in marketing your product and building your business, which can take time. The profits in a product business can be smaller than a service business, and you may have to sell lots of products to make a decent profit.

If you can outsource product production, storage, and shipping, you can enjoy more flexibility and build a business from anywhere. But if you have a physical shop, you need to be available for customers, which may limit your lifestyle options. However, with the right manufacturer and distribution system, you can grow your product business to be a household name.

Here are some of the pros and cons of starting a product business:

Pros:

- ✗ Can create and sell a product, which can be very rewarding.
- ✗ Have access to a large global consumer market.
- ✗ Can sell products all the time.

✗ Can sell a variety of different products.

✗ Are not always reliant on your time.

Cons:

✗ Starting a product business can be a significant financial investment.

✗ The profit margins can be small.

✗ May need to sell a lot of products to make a decent profit.

✗ The market can dictate the price of your product.

✗ Often need to work with other people to produce, store, and distribute your product.

Network Marketing Business

Networking marketing – also known as direct sales, multi-level marketing (MLM), or social marketing – is another type of business you can start. Alongside my freelance work, in the early days of finding my way in the business world, I also had a network marketing business. I learned so much, earned money, and met some wonderful people.

In network marketing, you sell a company's product and receive a commission. You can also recruit other people into your business, where you are known as the upline and they are the downline. You can earn a commission on your downline's sales as well.

Network marketing has often had a bad reputation due to the perception that you have to recruit as many people as possible. This may have put some people off, and there are many preconceived ideas, such as it's "just for moms" or it's a "little side business". However, I have met a lot of people making extremely large incomes in network marketing, but it's not for everyone.

I loved my time in my networking marketing business. We received so much free training, and I attended conferences where I was inspired and learned so much. I built my business to a good level, but I found it difficult to maintain, especially as I began to have other business interests. However, I've been able to take a lot of what I learned and apply it to my other businesses.

In network marketing, you would usually be a sole trader and have to register for taxes like any business, but you receive payment directly from the parent company you have aligned yourself with.

Network marketing can be a wonderful business for so many people, especially those with little prior business knowledge, and it's a great way to connect with other people who have a similar mindset to you. You receive mentoring, but the quality can vary depending on your upline (this is the person who introduced you to the business and then the person who introduced them, etc.).

One thing I didn't like about networking marketing is that you are not a decision-maker in the business, and you don't always know what is happening within the company. So although you have your business, there were elements to me that felt like a corporate company which still has a hierarchy.

Something you will find with most network marketing businesses is they have high-quality products, and although I don't actively build my business now, I still love the nutrition products that I used to sell.

Network marketing aligns itself with the laptop lifestyle of living and working from anywhere, but it's not always the case, especially if you want to lead with samples or you're in a country where the products are not available. However, that doesn't mean you can't meet with people from countries where it is available and then send them products or information at a later date.

Network marketing is often sold on being able to build in a small amount of time each week, but this isn't usually the case. You have to put in the time and effort to receive the reward.

Here are some pros and cons of network marketing:

Pros:

- All the products are created for you.

- The commissions are paid directly to you.

- You usually receive high-level training.

- Can meet some wonderful people.

- High-end good quality products.

- Repeat customers and downline can mean repeat income.

- Low start-up cost.

Cons:

- The industry has a negative reputation.

- No control over products.

- Always having to find new people to join the business.

- Can be pressure from your upline to grow.

- You're not a decision-maker in the company.

- Investment in products can be high if you want to try them.

If you are considering network marketing, here are some recommendations:

1. **Do your research:** Before joining any network marketing company, do your due diligence and thoroughly research the company, its products, and its compensation plan. Look for reviews and feedback from other distributors and customers, and make sure the company is legitimate and has a good reputation.

2. **Choose a company that aligns with your values:** Make sure the products and the company's mission align with your values and interests. This will help you stay motivated and passionate about your business.

3. **Build a strong network:** Your success in network marketing depends on building a strong network of customers and distributors. Focus on building relationships with people and providing value to them, rather than just trying to recruit them into your business.

4. **Don't pressure people:** Avoid pressuring people to join your business or buy your products. Instead, focus on educating them about the benefits of the products and how they can help improve their lives.

5. **Invest in your personal development:** Network marketing can be challenging, so it's important to invest in your personal development and mindset. Attend training

events, read books, and listen to podcasts to continually improve your skills and knowledge.

6. **Be consistent:** Consistency is key in network marketing. Set aside time each week to work on your business and stick to it. Even if you only have a few hours a week to dedicate to your business, stay consistent and focus on the most important tasks.

7. **Be patient:** Building a successful network marketing business takes time and effort. Don't expect overnight success and be prepared to put in the work over the long term. With patience and persistence, you can build a thriving business and achieve your goals.

In just a few pages, I have provided an overview of the different types of businesses that you can start. You can either create a service- or product-based business from scratch or join an established network marketing company.

I understand that it can be overwhelming to consider all the possibilities available to you, but building a business can also be exciting and rewarding. In the upcoming chapters, I will guide you in determining which type of business is suitable for you at the moment, and how you can eventually create multiple businesses and income streams.

N N N

What to focus on:

✗ **Embrace Diverse Career Paths:** Recognise the various business opportunities available to you, from traditional professions to creative ventures.

✗ **Build a Business with Your Personality:** Choose a business that fits your personality, strengths, and interests for greater success and satisfaction.

✗ **Service-Based Business:** Allow you to use your current skills and create a business which can be flexible to you.

✗ **Product-Based Business:** Create something to sell to the world. This is likely to require more financial investment.

"The most important thing is to enjoy your life — to be happy — it's all that matters."

Audrey Hepburn

CHAPTER 4

HOW DO I KNOW WHAT IS RIGHT FOR ME?

After reading through the previous chapters, you might be feeling a bit overwhelmed and uncertain about your business or business idea. Perhaps you're wondering if you're on the right track or if you need to start over. Take a deep breath and don't panic!

In this chapter, I'll guide you and provide some reassurance. With so many business options out there, it's perfectly normal to feel uncertain. If you're like me and never had a clear sense of life's purpose, that's okay too. I had friends in school who knew exactly what they wanted to do, went to university to study it, and are still on that career path. But for some of us, finding our path is a bit more challenging.

A life purpose – or not

It's important not to believe that there is only one thing you are meant to do in life. You can do many things and enjoy them along the way. This belief will take the pressure off. You don't have to feel like you need to be chasing after a calling or that every decision you make in your business needs to be overly analysed. Each of us has specific skills and personality traits that make us come alive. When you find something that fits you and your skills, you're on to a winner!

I don't believe that we all have to have a single true life purpose. Instead, you can shift and change your career as you develop and grow as a person. That's what I've done, and I have to admit it's been a pretty fun journey so far!

Although you might not have a specific purpose, you might find that there is a common thread throughout your life. It could be that you have always been creative and made things with your hands in different ways over the years. Or you might love to help people and have had jobs that do exactly that.

What do you do?

The goal for you now is to find something that brings you joy – something you could talk about all day long and that you love, which aligns with who you are and the personality profile you discovered in the previous chapters.

One of the reasons I love working for myself is because I came from a place of pain. I felt lost, didn't enjoy my job, and felt like

I would be stuck working in the 9 to 5 forever. I would have a pity party every Sunday, often shedding a few tears because I didn't want to go to the office the next day. Since I decided to work for myself, I've never looked back. Although I have pivoted quite a few times, and it's certainly not always been easy, I know that I don't want to go back to that place, and I don't want you to either.

No matter what you are doing now, you will never stop learning in business. You will always be improving, learning, and evolving as a businesswoman. Your business is such a big part of your life that it should be important to you. I am not saying it has to be 'life-changing', but it needs to be aligned with you, something that you enjoy, and something that means you can't wait to jump out of bed to do each morning.

If you have already started your business and you feel like it does complement your personality, then that's wonderful – keep going. This will give you a great base to start from and is something you can build on.

If you're still not sure what to do, pick something from the last chapter, like a service you can offer or a product you can sell, which will give you a starting point. There is no better time than today to get started and take the first step.

It's important to ask yourself, how does what I am doing work for with me, and how can I do it better?

My first ever job was a fairly mundane data entry role. At first, it was exciting to earn money, but that soon wore off. I loved the people I worked with (mostly), but there was a guilt that I didn't run into the office with a hop, skip, and a jump. I probably didn't smile until mid-morning when the trolley came around with bacon sandwiches – that was certainly a highlight of each day! Thinking back, I don't know why I felt guilty; inputting words and numbers into a computer all day is not going to fill many people with joy, especially someone with untapped ambition and creativity.

In the last chapter, I shared how there are so many different businesses you can start. What I don't want is for you to now get analysis paralysis and worry about not picking the 'right' business. This is just a way of putting off and letting your doubts creep in. I have met so many women over the years who are stuck to waiting for the best time or to receive some kind of divine message to help them find their calling. I recently heard that procrastination is just fear, and I can relate to that. Every time I find myself putting something off, it's usually because I am worried about the outcome. Almost all of the time, there is absolutely no need to worry either!

Choosing a business should be a joy, and if it turns out that it isn't, then you can always change it.

When I decided to write a book, I felt like there were so many topics I wanted to discuss that it was overwhelming – how could I fit everything I love into one book? A mentor of mine reminded me how I can write multiple books around the different subjects and then all of a sudden, I was committed to the topic of helping you build a business that connects with who you are. I did this knowing that if I wanted to cover other subjects in the future, then that would be fine and it took the pressure off me.

> Pick something that will bring you joy. This is so important!

If you do create a business which you find that you don't love or it just doesn't work for you, then you can change it. You will naturally want to anyway. Have you got this message yet?

Pick something that will bring you joy. This is so important!

Business starts with your passion

Passion is the driving force behind any successful business. When you're passionate about what you do, it shows in your work, social media posts, and interactions with clients. Your enthusiasm sets you apart from the competition, making your business unique and authentic.

Running a business can be challenging, and it's not for everyone. However, if you enjoy what you do, it will keep you motivated and focused, even when faced with challenges. If you're not feeling good about something in your business, it's time to make a change. You make the rules in your business, so you have the power to pour your love and excitement into it.

Enthusiasm for your business is what will get you ahead of the competition.

Find what you're enthusiastic about, and build a business that you love. Although there may be tasks you don't love doing in any business, overall, you want to do something that you enjoy.

Your enthusiasm will help you stand out in your industry, and it will keep you motivated to keep going.

Enthusiasm for your business is what will get you ahead of the competition.

Building a business that you love empowers you to change your industry and share your excitement with the world. When you're excited about your business, you can't help but talk about it. Your enthusiasm will attract others to your business, and they will be drawn to your authentic passion.

Your business will evolve naturally over time. Keep it exciting by adding new projects or businesses that align with your interests and personality. Always keep your business evolving to keep things fresh and exciting.

Ask yourself these questions to help you identify what you're passionate about and what type of business to start:

✗ What interests do I have?

✗ What previous knowledge do I have?

✗ What equipment is required to start?

✗ What budget do I have?

✗ Is there anything I've always wanted to start?

✗ What lifestyle do I want to create?

✗ What time and other commitments do I have?

✗ What personality traits did I discover in the earlier chapter?

There are so many opportunities in today's world, but it's essential not to spread yourself too thin. In the next chapter, you'll learn about building multiple income streams and how to do it in a way that works for you. By taking small steps, you can continue to enjoy everything that you do while building your dream business.

✗ ✗ ✗

What to focus on:

↗ **Embrace Uncertainty in Business Choices:** If you are feeling overwhelmed or unsure about your business direction, this is normal. Remember, it's okay not to have a clear life purpose or a single career path.

↗ **Life Purpose Flexibility:** Understand that your life purpose can evolve. You don't need to be confined to one specific calling. Look for common themes in your interests and experiences.

↗ **Finding Joy in Your Work:** Look for business activities that bring you joy, and work with your personality traits and skills. This will lead to more fulfilling work.

↗ **The Importance of Passion:** Passion is crucial in business. It drives success, sets you apart, and helps you overcome challenges. Ensure your business reflects your passions and interests.

↗ **Changing Direction is Acceptable:** Don't fear starting over or pivoting your business if it doesn't bring joy or fit with your long-term vision. Business evolution is a natural and necessary part of growth.

"And the day came when the risk to remain tight in a bud was more painful than the risk it took to blossom."

Anaïs Nin

CHAPTER 5

MULTIPLE INCOME STREAMS

With all the different business opportunities out there, you may have a plethora of new ideas. However, it's essential to have a clear idea of the direction you want your business to go. Don't rush into everything just yet. Having said that, it doesn't mean you have to stick to one income stream. You just need to make sure that it is the right direction for you and your business and that you can keep the quality high in all your business areas.

In this chapter, I'll show you how to build multiple income streams, either as separate businesses or as part of the business you already have.

One crucial thing to consider when adding anything new is whether it excites and motivates you. Also, you need to know whether it can create an income for you, which is crucial when expanding your business and life, and also whether it is manageable for you on top of your existing business.

Here are some benefits of having multiple income streams:

✗ **Financial Security:** Provides a sense of financial security. If one income source is affected, you can rely on other income streams.

✗ **Diversification:** Allows you to diversify your income sources, giving you variety in your work and reducing the risk of relying on a single source of income.

✗ **Increased Income:** Can help you earn more money overall, which can be used for savings, investments, and paying off debts.

✗ **Greater Control:** You have more control over your financial situation as you are not reliant on a single client or product.

✗ **Flexibility:** Gives you more flexibility in how you earn money and manage your time.

✗ **Opportunities for Growth:** Provides opportunities for growth as you can explore different ways to earn money and use what you've learned across your different businesses or projects.

✗ **Better Work-Life Balance:** Creates a better work-life balance by adjusting your income streams to fit your schedule and priorities.

✗ **Personal Development:** Provides opportunities for personal development as you learn new skills and explore new ideas.

✗ **Increased Happiness:** Can increase your overall happiness by allowing you to pursue your passions and interests.

It's great to have lots of ideas, especially for creative business owners. Some ideas may never come to fruition, but many can. The key is to take it one step at a time.

The most important factor to consider before adding anything to your business is time. Your time is incredibly valuable. If you plan to add something new to your business or start another business, you must have enough time for it. You will also need to decide whether you want to invest some of your time in the new project.

Questions to ask yourself

Before you add any new project to your business, there are a few questions you need to answer.

Firstly, what is the time investment going to be? Will it be something you can integrate into your existing business or will you need to establish a new brand? Is it a quick project or will it take longer? Do you want it to be the same size and effort as your current business? Do you need to find additional support or do you already have a team who can help?

Then ask yourself if this new project will bring you joy and if you are enthusiastic about it. Also, how much money can it potentially make? Is it something that can be scaled and built over time? Will it compliment your current brand and build more awareness?

After the events of 2020, I am even more passionate about the importance of having multiple income streams. Whether they are all part of one business or different businesses, it is crucial to have multiple ways of making money. The pandemic reminded us that businesses need to be flexible and adaptable. If you are relying on just one income stream, any disruption could bring your business to an unexpected stop.

To ensure that any new project or business venture is successful, it must be profitable. As an established business owner, everything you do must have the potential to make money. it's also important to remain enthusiastic about your current projects and ensure that you have enough time

Different businesses may have different busy seasons.

to devote to them. You don't want to abandon what you are doing; instead, you need to find balance and ensure that all your projects receive the time and energy they deserve.

Different businesses may have different busy seasons. For

example, in a service business, the New Year and spring may be busy, while in ecommerce, the build-up to Christmas is usually the peak period. By knowing the income trends of your businesses in advance, you can plan your time more effectively and ensure consistent income throughout the year.

Types of additional income streams

Adding new projects to your current business is a great way to create an additional income stream. Here are some ideas to consider:

Service Business:

If you have a service business, there are plenty of ways to increase revenue within that business alone. One option is to offer additional services if you have the capacity. It's beneficial to have different service options at various price points so that you can attract a broader range of clients.

You could also create courses or coaching programs about your service. Don't assume that people don't want to learn your skills; there is a demand for online courses on various topics, and this could be an opportunity to share your expertise with a broader audience. Once a course is created, it can generate revenue for years to come.

Another option is to create physical products related to your service. For example, if you are a yoga teacher, you could sell yoga mats, clothing, or other accessories that your clients would appreciate. Be creative with your products and make sure they fit with your brand and audience.

Product Business:

If you have a product-based business, you can also offer coaching or courses related to your product. If you are an artist, for example, you could teach people how to paint. This can provide additional revenue and help establish you as an authority in your field.

You could also offer services in addition to your products. For instance, if you design products, you could consider offering white-label services to other companies. This means creating or designing products for them without branding them as your own. This can be an excellent way to generate additional revenue without requiring additional resources.

Passive Income:

Creating passive income streams is another way to generate revenue. Passive income refers to money that you earn continuously without requiring ongoing effort. Examples of passive income include royalties from products or books, rental income, and affiliate marketing. However, it's important to remember that no business is truly passive. Even if a business runs automatically, it still requires maintenance, monitoring, and occasional updates.

Adding new projects to your business can be an excellent way to generate additional revenue. It's important to choose projects that align with your brand and expertise, and that fill you with enthusiasm. By doing this, you can create a multifaceted business that generates revenue from multiple sources.

A great example of this is my friend Susan, a business coach who helps new entrepreneurs set up their operations and find their first clients. She offers a range of packages, from 1-hour consultations to 6-month full-coaching programmes. She realised that not everyone wants her 1 to 1 programs so she created an online course. Susan packaged her expertise into a 6-week online course, covering everything from ideation to executing a business plan. Once created, this course became a valuable passive income stream for her. She markets this course as a self-paced alternative to her 1-on-1 coaching. Following this, she then created a physical planner that aids in task management, goal setting, and planning. It quickly gained popularity among her existing clients, and she eventually started selling it on her website and social media platforms.

By diversifying her income streams, Susan not only increased her revenue but also expanded her reach. Each component adds value to her brand, making it a cohesive ecosystem that continuously attracts a broad range of clients.

When to create a new business or brand

If you want to create something that is entirely different from your current business, I recommend creating a new brand. While I don't believe in strict niches, you don't want to confuse your customers. For example, if you are a solicitor who also sells handmade candles, you might want to keep these as separate entities because you are likely to have two very different customers with different interests, and maintaining different websites and marketing strategies for each would be the best option.

If you decide to set up a separate business, you will need to come up with a new name, website, grow a mailing list, and undertake all the other necessary steps for starting a new business. This can take up more time, energy, and finances to get started, but it can also be a lot of fun.

When you have already built a business, you have more experience, and you can use that experience to grow your new brand faster. You can take everything you have learned in creating your original business and apply it to your new one, which can make the process smoother and less daunting.

Outsourcing

Having multiple businesses or projects within your business can be overwhelming, and outsourcing can become your best friend. Outsourcing is all about delegating tasks to other people. My recommendation is to start small and find freelancers to do small projects for you.

Outsourcing tasks is a great way for small businesses to free up time and resources to focus on core business activities.

Here are some examples of work that can be outsourced by small businesses:

✗ **Bookkeeping and accounting:** Outsourcing financial tasks such as bookkeeping and accounting can help you stay on top of your finances.

✗ **Customer service:** Outsourcing customer service tasks such as answering phone calls and emails, managing social media accounts, and responding to customer enquiries can help small businesses provide high-quality customer service and can free up a lot of time.

✗ **Marketing and advertising:** Outsourcing marketing tasks such as website design, social media management, and advertising campaigns can help you increase brand awareness.

✗ **Human resources:** Outsourcing human resources tasks such as recruiting, hiring, and payroll management can help you manage your staff.

✗ **Graphic design and content creation:** Outsourcing graphic design tasks such as creating logos, designing marketing materials, and developing website content can help you create a professional image.

✗ **Legal services:** Outsourcing legal tasks such as contract drafting and review, trademark registration, and business formation can ensure legal compliance.

✗ **Administrative tasks:** Outsourcing administrative tasks such as data entry, appointment scheduling, and emails can streamline your business.

✗ **Research and analysis:** Outsourcing research and analysis tasks such as market research, and competitor analysis can help you make informed decisions.

It's important to maintain a healthy work/life balance when managing multiple income streams. If you're already struggling to manage your current business and personal life, then starting a new business or project may not be the best idea at the moment.

Take this as an opportunity to evaluate your current business and determine if there are tasks you can delegate to free up your time. It's easy to fall into the trap of thinking that you're the only one who can handle everything, but finding someone with the necessary skills can reduce the pressure and give you more time.

If you're not yet in a position to add another income stream to your business or start a new one, don't worry. Knowing that it's a possibility is already a step forward. You can always revisit the idea in the future when the timing is right for you. In the meantime, use this time to learn and prepare for your next venture.

If you're ready to take the plunge, pick a new project or start a new brand and go for it. I have faith in you, and I know that your hard work will pay off in the long run. Remember that having a business requires consistent experimentation and effort. Keep at it, and you'll reap the rewards.

N N N

What to focus on:

N Benefits of Multiple Income Streams: Diversifying income sources offers financial security, increased income potential, greater control over finances, better work-life balance, and opportunities for personal and professional growth.

✔ Evaluating Time Investment: Before adding new ventures, assess the time required. Ensure you can integrate them into your existing schedule or that you have the capacity to manage additional commitments.

✔ Key Questions to Consider: Reflect on the potential time investment, alignment with existing business, scale of effort, and financial prospects of new projects. Assess whether these align with your joy and enthusiasm.

✔ Profitability and Passion in New Ventures: Ensure new ventures are not only profitable but also work with your current interests and commitments. Balance is key to managing multiple businesses or projects.

✔ Seasonal Trends and Planning: Understand and anticipate the busy seasons in different business types for effective planning and consistent income.

✔ Ideas for Additional Income Streams: Explore various methods to expand your business, including offering additional services, creating online courses, selling physical products related to your services, or engaging in passive income activities like affiliate marketing.

✔ Deciding to Create a New Brand: If your new project is distinctly different from your current business, consider establishing a separate brand to avoid customer confusion.

"Better to live one year as a tiger, than a hundred as a sheep."

Madonna

CHAPTER 6
BE CREATIVE IN YOUR BUSINESS

By now, you should have a clear idea of what your business is about, and the different income streams and projects you want to pursue. Hopefully, you've found something that ignites your passion. Now, it's time to start getting creative in your business.

Regardless of your business or personality type, incorporating creativity is essential to help you stand out. You might not consider yourself a creative person, but that doesn't mean you should dismiss the idea of bringing creativity into your business. Creativity is not only limited to the arts. There are many ways to be creative in your business, and it can make a significant impact on your success.

Personally, I never thought of myself as a creative person when I was younger. I even got a D in my art GCSE, which made me believe I wasn't arty or creative. However, as I got older, I realised that creativity comes in many different forms. I completed my degree in creative writing, and I started to use my creativity in the stories I was telling, the blog posts I was creating, and on social media.

Here are a few ways you can bring creativity into your business:

- ↗ Generating ideas for new products or services.

- ↗ Exploring innovative ways to bring new products or services to market.

- ↗ Creating unique marketing materials and advertisements.

- ↗ Developing engaging social media content.

- ↗ Crafting compelling blog posts.

- ↗ Writing captivating emails.

- ↗ Producing high-quality photos and videos.

- ↗ Identifying opportunities for collaborations with others.

Incorporating creativity into your business may feel daunting, but it can also be an enjoyable and rewarding experience. So, don't be afraid to think outside the box and try new things. Your business and customers will thank you for it.

Get into the creative zone

When it comes to being creative – especially if it doesn't come naturally or you are feeling a bit blocked when it comes to ideas – you can do lots of different things to help you get into 'the zone'.

Change your environment: This is one I do a lot; it's easy when working from home as I can move from one room to another or head to a local coffee shop or hotel lobby if I need a complete change. Having somewhere you feel comfortable spending a few hours can help you focus.

Tidy your work area: If you're like me and allow things to get messy, then spend 15 minutes giving your desk a tidy up, perhaps even light a candle and then get focused. It's amazing how clearing a few papers away and getting rid of your empty coffee mug can have a big impact on getting into the zone.

Take a break: Sometimes it is hard to think of a new idea, especially when you try to force it. Allow yourself some time off – you could even take a holiday. It might sound a bit extreme but even a night away in a hotel can help you relax and then let the ideas flow! I know when I have been on holiday, I often come back full of fresh ideas so I always make sure to have a notebook and pen with me because you never know when a fun new idea might appear – I have had some of my best ideas sipping on a rum punch by the beach!

Find a way to relax: Even if booking a trip to the Caribbean is not an option today, you can still find a way to relax and switch off your mind to allow those new ideas to come in. Find out what helps you to relax the best. It could be a bath, a workout, a walk, time with friends or a massage. Try different things and see which works for you. The idea is to then come back to your business feeling rejuvenated and with some new ideas.

Try new ways to do things: If you always work on your laptop, try writing in a notebook or grab some coloured pens and go mad. If you are struggling to write, record your thoughts into your phone. Trying different things can help unlock a different part of your brain.

Some of these suggestions might sound a bit too easy. You might believe you will never come up with new ideas and be more creative but they can work. Sometimes you might need to try more than one thing, but trust yourself that you will be able to come up with some new creative ideas for your business.

Business Owner = Content Creator

As a business owner, especially of a small business, creating content is a critical aspect of marketing and promoting your business. In today's world, we all need to market our businesses, which means creating content for online or offline platforms.

A content creator is someone who produces informative, entertaining, and engaging content for their audience. This can include writing, videography, photography, graphic design, art and podcasting. Unless you can employ someone or outsource content creation from the very beginning, you will need to create content for your business at some point.

Even if you employ or outsource someone to create content, it's still a good idea for you to be involved in the creation process. You know your business best and can provide valuable insights into what type of content resonates with your target audience.

As a business owner, you may not thrive on creating content and posting on social media. But creating content is a way to market your business and attract potential clients and customers. When I first started in business, I created my website and expected people to contact me, which did not happen. It was then that I realised the importance of promoting my business by creating content.

With numerous social media platforms available, you can create and publish content for free. While paid advertising is a great way to reach a wider audience, using free social media platforms should be your priority when starting out.

You do not need to be on every platform in the beginning; start by finding the platform where your customers are and where you feel the most comfortable. As you gain more confidence and experience, you can expand to other platforms.

Creating content can be done using your phone or computer, and it presents a great opportunity to get creative and try new things out. Remember, you are the content creator for your business, and your unique perspective and knowledge are valuable assets that can help you connect with your target audience.

Get inspired

If creating content doesn't come naturally to you, then research can be your best friend. Priming your brain to look at what content is out there and thinking of ways you can utilise it to fit your business will help.

Spend time each week looking at what content is out there. What are people in a similar industry sharing? What are top accounts in different niches doing? What type of content seems to be popular right now? Ask yourself these questions and then see how you can incorporate what you see into your business.

This isn't about copying, although on some social media platforms, there can be trends that mean you might do something similar. Instead, it's about bringing popular content concepts into your brand.

Doing this research can help you make creating content fun. I don't want you to see it as a mundane task that has to be done. Inject your personality into the content you create.

Even if you decide to outsource your content in the future (or right now), I would encourage you to continue doing research and come up with ideas for your brand, even if you pay someone else to execute them for you. This way, you can be part of the process and understand what can work for your business and what might not, especially if you are the face of your brand.

Social media is not going away anytime soon, so the more understanding you have around what's working means you can put your brand out there effectively.

Content Types

There are four main types of content that businesses should create: writing, photography, audio and video. In today's world, you can create all of this content from your smartphone or laptop without needing a lot of professional equipment. As your business and skills grow, you can invest in equipment, but it's not recommended to invest in too much equipment early on, as you won't know exactly what you need until you start creating content.

Writing is the type of content you will create the most. You'll write for your website, blog posts, captions on social media, product descriptions, sales pages, and emails. Finding your brand voice is crucial when writing. Keep it chatty and relaxed, and aim to make your brand feel approachable. If you're unsure about your writing, ask someone else to read it out loud or read it out yourself. Reading your work aloud can help you to naturally change and improve what you've written. Make sure to also check your spelling and grammar, and get someone to check over your work if you're unsure.

Photography is essential for visual branding. You can use the camera on your phone to take great quality photos, and there are many apps available for editing images. Always take lots of photos and experiment with different styles, including candid images. Don't forget to put your phone away to enjoy the moment too.

Video is another visual medium that has grown dramatically over the years. Videos on your website and social media platforms can help you connect with your customers. You can create tutorials, vlogs, information videos, lessons, and product videos. You don't have to appear on camera if you don't want to. Keep it simple and use your phone to record videos. Editing apps can also help you create professional-looking videos. Remember to keep your videos to the point and try to cut back on filler phrases such as "um" and "you know." Over time, you'll improve and notice a difference.

Audio content is another valuable form of content that businesses should consider incorporating into their strategies. Whether it's podcasts, audio blogs, or even voice snippets on social media, audio offers a personal, direct way to connect with your audience. Much like video and writing, audio can be produced without any high-end equipment; a good quality smartphone microphone may be sufficient for starting out. The intimacy of your voice allows you to engage your audience in a different, often deeper, way compared to written or visual content. It can also be more accessible; people can listen while they're driving, working out, or doing chores, giving you more opportunities to reach them. As you grow, you may choose to invest in specialised microphones or editing software to enhance the audio experience. But the most important factor, regardless of the equipment you use, is the value and authenticity you bring through your spoken words.

Batching Content

One of my favourite ways to create content is by batching it. Batching content is the process of creating multiple pieces of content at one time, rather than creating each piece individually as it is needed.

Here are some reasons why you should batch content:

- **✗ Time-saving:** Can save you time by allowing you to create multiple pieces of content in one sitting. This can help you avoid the time-consuming process of starting and stopping each time you need to create new content.

- **✗ Consistency:** Helps maintain a consistent posting schedule by creating a stockpile of content that you can publish over time. This can help you avoid gaps in your content schedule.

- **✗ Efficiency:** Streamlines your workflow by allowing you to focus on one type of task at a time. This can help you avoid distractions and increase your overall efficiency.

↗ **Flexibility:** More flexibility with your schedule by allowing you to create content in advance and schedule it to be published at a later date. This can help you avoid last-minute scrambling to create content.

Here are some tips for batching content:

↗ **Plan ahead:** Before you start, create a plan for what types of content you want to create and how you will use it.

↗ **Schedule time:** Set aside dedicated time and treat it as an important part of your schedule.

↗ **Stay organised:** Keep track of the content you create, including the topic, format, and date of creation.

↗ **Use templates:** Use templates for blog posts, social media posts, and other types of content to save time and ensure consistency.

↗ **Edit later:** When you are batching content, focus on creating the content itself rather than editing it. You can go back and edit later to ensure quality.

Managing your social media content

Social media has become such an important part of the business landscape. Here are my top tips of managing your social media, taken from my time as a social media manager!

1. **Define your social media strategy:** Before you start posting on social media, define your goals, target audience, and key messages. This will help ensure that your social media efforts are aligned with your overall business strategy.

2. **Choose the right platforms:** Focus on the social media platforms where your target audience is most active. Don't try to be active on every platform – it's better to do a few things well than to do many things poorly. This is especially true at the beginning of your business. Later, you can expand to other platforms.

3. **Develop a content calendar:** Create a content calendar to plan your social media posts in advance. This will help you maintain a consistent posting schedule and ensure that your content is diverse and engaging.

4. **Engage with your audience:** Social media is a two-way conversation, so make sure to respond to comments, questions, and messages from your audience. This will help build a sense of community and improve your brand's reputation.

5. **Monitor your metrics:** Keep track of your social media metrics, such as follower growth, engagement rates, and click-through rates. Use this information to refine your strategy and improve your content over time.

6. **Use automation tools:** There are many social media automation tools available that can help you save time and streamline your social media management. These tools can help you schedule posts in advance, monitor your brand's reputation, and track your metrics.

7. **Stay up-to-date:** Social media is constantly evolving, so make sure to stay up-to-date on the latest trends and changes. Attend industry conferences, read industry blogs and newsletters, networking with fellow business owners and follow social media thought leaders to stay informed.

By following these tips, you can effectively manage your social media and use it to build your brand, engage with your audience, and drive business results.

Keep it fun

Creating content can be a fun and rewarding experience if you approach it with the right mindset and don't overthink what you're doing. Remember, you can always delete something if it doesn't work out. Content creation is a fantastic opportunity to get your business in front of people who may not have known about you otherwise, so it's important to take advantage of it.

However, it's important not to dive in and try to do everything at once. Learning, improving, and growing should be your motto when creating content for your business. Take it one step at a time, and don't be afraid to experiment and try new things. With practice, you'll find your own unique voice and style that resonates with your audience. So embrace the process and have fun with getting creative within your business. Think outside the box, be inspired and create content that you enjoy.

✗ ✗ ✗

What to focus on:

✗ Embrace Creativity in Business: Regardless of your self-perceived creativity level, finding innovative ways to stand out is vital for business success.

✗ Role as a Content Creator: As a small business owner, producing diverse content is key for your marketing and audience engagement. Start with accessible platforms and tools, gradually expanding your reach.

✗ Research for Inspiration: Regularly explore content in your industry and beyond for ideas. Adapt popular concepts to fit your brand, maintaining authenticity.

✗ Diverse Content Types: Focus on creating written, photographic, audio, and video content. Start with basic tools like smartphones and laptops, upgrading equipment as needed.

✗ Content Batching Benefits: Batching content creation saves time, ensures consistency, and streamlines workflow. Plan, organise and schedule content production effectively.

↗ Effective Social Media Management: Define a clear social media strategy, select appropriate platforms, develop a content calendar, engage with your audience, monitor metrics, use automation tools, and stay informed about social media trends.

↗ Enjoy the Creative Process: Approach content creation with a fun, experimental mindset. Learn, improve, and grow in your style and approach, making content creation an enjoyable part of your business journey.

"The most effective way to do it, is to do it."

Amelia Earhart

CHAPTER 7
WHAT DOES SUCCESS MEAN TO YOU?

Success is a term that's often thrown around in the business community, and it's something that you undoubtedly strive for when you start your own business. However, the meaning of success can vary widely from person to person.

When you break it down, success is a highly personal and subjective concept. Your definition of success might differ from that of your peers, or even from day to day, depending on where you are in your life journey. In this chapter, we will explore the various measures of success and help you identify which ones resonate most with you.

It's important to note that success is not just about making money. While financial success is often seen as the ultimate goal, it's not the only way to achieve success. The Oxford Dictionary defines success as "the accomplishment of an aim or purpose," which means that you get to decide what success looks like for you.

So, take a moment to reflect on what success means to you. Jot down your initial thoughts and consider how they may change depending on the circumstances.

By exploring the different ways in which you can be successful in your business, you'll be better equipped to stay motivated and focused, even when doubts creep in.

Different types of success

Let's explore the various types of success that you can achieve in your business:

Financial success is undoubtedly the most obvious measure of success. However, it's important to remember that your financial aims should be realistic and achievable, based on your unique circumstances. While it's important to make money, focusing solely on financial success can be a double-edged sword. You might find yourself perpetually unsatisfied and always wanting more, even if you've hit your monetary targets.

Lifestyle is another key measure of success. Building a business that allows you to live the life you want is a major achievement. Whether it's spending more time with your family or taking time off to travel, your ability to create the lifestyle you desire is a key indicator of success.

Joy is perhaps the most overlooked measure of success.

Building a business that brings you happiness and fulfilment should be a primary goal. After all, what's the point of building a successful business if you're miserable every day? Finding joy in your work and feeling excited to wake up every morning to tackle new challenges is a significant measure of success.

Ultimately, the goal should be to achieve success in all of these categories. By making money, creating the lifestyle you desire, and finding joy in your work, you'll be on the path to achieving true success. While not every day will be perfect, striving for more successful moments than not will help you to look back on your journey with pride and a sense of accomplishment. Remember to stay focused on your passion and enjoy the journey of building your business.

Your business success

I believe in having a clear direction for your business, but I don't necessarily advocate for traditional goal-setting methods. Writing down a goal with a specific deadline can sometimes feel too restrictive, and if you don't achieve it, you might feel disappointed instead of proud of your progress. Instead, I prefer to have a vision for where I want my business to go, including what I want my role to be, which products I want to create, and the lifestyle I want to build. Money is also an important factor, but it's not the only measure of success.

Visualising my 'end scene' motivates me to work towards my vision every day. In the Mindset chapter, I'll share more about how to do this effectively.

Only you know what your ultimate goal is.

For now, I encourage you to dream big and write down your ultimate business success without worrying about the details or setting a deadline. What does success look like to you? It could be paying off your mortgage, moving to a bigger office with a team, winning a business award, or taking your family on a dream vacation. Only you know what your ultimate goal is.

By having a clear vision for your business, you can remove some of the immediate pressure and make better decisions. Every task you do should be aligned with your ultimate goal. It's important to remember that your definition of success may be different from others, and that's okay. Stay focused on your own journey, surround yourself with positive influences, and stay true to who you are and what you want to achieve.

Celebrate your successes

To develop a success-oriented mindset, it's important to celebrate even the small achievements that are propelling your business forward. Celebration doesn't necessarily have to involve extravagant parties or expensive gifts – if you're like me, a glass of fizz always hits the spot. You can acknowledge your accomplishments by treating yourself to something you enjoy or simply patting yourself on the back mentally.

For instance, when my friend Jenny's yoga studio celebrated its first anniversary, she threw a big party with food, drinks and dancers to thank all those who had supported her. Jenny was proud of what she had accomplished in that year and wanted to share her joy with others. The added benefit was that she could use the event to publicise the studio in the local press and generate fresh content for her online platforms.

The beauty of entrepreneurship is that you get to define your own version of success, celebrate it however you like, and create the life you want. Success is an ever-evolving concept, and as you attain your goals, you'll set new ones and continue growing your business. You may even decide to change direction altogether, and that's okay too! The important thing is to keep celebrating your progress and accomplishments.

Remember, don't allow external factors to determine your definition of success. Only you can decide what success means for you, and I'm confident that you can achieve all the success you desire.

и и и

What to focus on:

✗ Personal Nature of Success: Understand that success is a subjective concept, varying between different people. It's essential to define what success means to you personally

✗ Beyond Financial Gains: While financial success is a common goal, it should not be the sole measure of success. True success encompasses a range of factors including lifestyle, personal fulfilment, and joy in your work.

✗ Celebrating Successes: Recognise and celebrate achievements, big or small. Celebrations can be simple acknowledgments or larger events, but the key is to appreciate your progress and milestones.

✗ Individual Journey and Growth: Embrace the uniqueness of your success journey. Avoid comparing your progress to others and stay true to your personal definition of success. Be open to evolving your goals and changing direction as your business grows.

"Success isn't about how much money you make, it's about the difference you make in people's lives."

Michelle Obama

CHAPTER 8
SETTING YOURSELF UP FOR SUCCESS

In the previous chapter, we discussed the importance of defining success on your own terms, which can change as you and your business grow. For example, a goal that was once a priority might become less important as your business shifts its focus or as your personal circumstances change.

For me, one way I've set myself up for success is by taking a break during the summer months. In doing so, I've had to let go of some of my regular business tasks, like consistent social media posting. But by prioritising rest and relaxation during this time, I've been able to celebrate a different kind of success that fits well with my personal goals.

Regardless of what stage your business is in, it's crucial to set yourself up for success. Take a moment to envision the successful business owner you want to be and think about how she would approach her day-to-day tasks. Then, start taking steps to embody that version of yourself.

One thing is certain: you should always be looking to set yourself up for success, no matter what stage of your business is at.

Think about the successful business owner you want to be and embody her.

How would she plan the day, execute a task or think about something?

Make a note now of how you see yourself in the future and start deciding how you can be her (or move towards being her) now.

As discussed earlier, there are lots of ways you can measure your success. Think back to the previous chapter when you decided what success means to you.

Here are some of my personal factors of success. I will go through each one and what I have learned so you can aim for it too.

- ✗ Having joy
- ✗ Freedom
- ✗ Financial
- ✗ Visibility
- ✗ Sense of achievement

Setting Yourself up for Success

Having joy

It might sound simple but there are so many business owners that are not having any fun in their business or even their life. They are so focused on the stress, the grind and the constant pushing involved in running a business that they never stop to see what they have built. I don't want that for you.

One of the key elements of this book has been to find a business which brings you joy and allows you to use your passion. Having joy in your business doesn't mean everything will be perfect but it does mean you can enjoy what you are doing for the majority of the time.

To build a successful business (in every way) means you have to spend time doing it. You might as well spend your time having fun, don't you agree?!

I know not every task will be fun and you won't be loving every single moment. However, if you can get out of bed most mornings and look forward to running your business, then you know you have done something right and found a great business for you.

On the days that you are not doing something you love, try to make it more fun! As a creative, I will always say doing my accounts is the least fun part of my business. That or someone wanting to talk to me on the phone – Hello, I'm a 'please don't call me because I'm a Millennial' over here!

But when, as a responsible business owner, I work on my accounts and finances, I do what I can to make it fun. This usually means blasting out some upbeat music, which always lifts my mood, and taking regular dance breaks to stop it from being so draining for me. Once I've done the finance tasks, I know I will feel so good so I make sure I keep telling myself that too!

It's a way of finding some joy in even the most boring (to me) tasks. When you have your own 'boring to you' work to do, find a way to make yourself smile!

As a business owner, it's okay for you to feel joy too. Give yourself permission to have fun. The business world can often be very serious but it doesn't have to be. Remember this is your business and you have every right to do it your way.

I am going to repeat it: it is okay for you to feel joy and have fun, even in your business.

You deserve to have joy. You are worthy of having joy. So, go for it.

As you build a business, you will spend a lot of time working on it and in it, so please remind yourself that you are more than worthy to do something you love. Although you will spend a long time working on your business, you do not need to spend every minute of every day working. It is okay to take breaks, time off and go and do things. Spend the money you are earning!

I don't condone hustle culture, which is often mentioned on social media. This is the culture of shaming business owners who are not constantly working on their business 24/7, working weekends, evenings and holidays. It's almost become a badge of honour to show how busy they are. This is not what I want for you and I'm pretty sure it's not what you want for yourself.

I don't want you to ever feel guilty for not subscribing to this culture of always working. The chances are, you have other commitments in your life so never, ever feel bad for not always working. Yes, it might mean you build the business at a slower pace but it might not be the case. If you come into your business working time feeling fresh and ready to go you will probably find you work more efficiently and have even better ideas.

Remember the last time you took an afternoon or day off for a spa day, or to go for a walk, or even just to meet up with a friend for a coffee and a chat? How much more positive and energised did you feel afterwards?

I know it is sometimes hard to do something else when it seems that the work is piling up while you are 'out of office', but believe me, when you get back, you will be a much better and more efficient and effective version of yourself.

When you are doing what you love, there is a chance you will work more than you intend and there will be times when it is hard to step away from your computer. Make sure you keep on top of this and remind yourself to keep finding joy in other areas of your life.

Trust me, taking regular breaks, not working constantly, and when you do work, being focused and doing it in a way which feels good to you will be much more effective for you. Create a schedule of your planned time off. This could be a family holiday you've already planned or setting aside a specific half-day each week to engage in an activity you love. Write down these plans and make sure to follow through on taking a break to enjoy yourself!

Freedom

The other benefit of not subscribing to hustle culture and working 24/7 means that you can create freedom in your business. For me, this is the opportunity to do what you want when you want! Now, you might not want to always be doing things away from your business, but having the possibility of doing it is a huge part of the success to me.

Freedom in your business allows you to create your rules and make your own decisions. You might want to work from different locations or set your own schedule. This means you can structure your day and your work to your life and other commitments which suits you.

Having freedom will help bring you more joy and can also help you to be more creative and achieve more success.

Creating freedom in your business takes time. At the beginning of your business, there will be lots for you to do as you start to grow. Don't let this stop you from planning your location and time freedom in the future. Set things up from the start which will help. A great example of this can be scheduling your content.

If having freedom is important to you, then it is possible for you.

For me, having freedom in my business means I can do things when I want. Just this last week, I did a few hours of work on a Sunday because I had no other plans, and there was some work I wanted to do. Then on Monday, I took the afternoon off to go to the cinema.

This is freedom for me.

Being able to build a flexible work schedule around the things I love and want to do. This is especially vital if you have other commitments in life. Freedom from your business can also help support these other responsibilities, such as picking children up from school, going to the gym or even caring for a parent. It can also give you availability for the things you want to do, such as meeting friends or hobbies.

A quick reminder – just because you can create freedom and flexibility in your business, it doesn't mean you always have to be available to friends or family either!

Being a business owner means you don't have to work a traditional 9 to 5. The chances are you started your business to get away from this so don't create a new 9 to 5 in your business.

Take advantage of creating your own rules, in a way which suits you, your personality and your lifestyle.

Not all businesses are the same. Yes, you might have a business where you need to be available during certain times of the day to speak to clients, but you can set this schedule.

When you let people know your availability and create your own rules, you will be surprised how people will comply! The key to this is doing it early on.

In service-based businesses where you work with clients, you need to be clear about your schedule and availability to them. Think about what you want for a moment. You might be happy to catch up on client work on a Sunday morning but mark

Tuesdays as a day you are unavailable to clients.

What I want you to do is find what suits you and stick with it!

For a product-based business, you can have an automatic reply to customer service emails to give yourself 24 to 48 hours to reply – or again, whatever suits you. This way, even if something comes in, you don't need to respond immediately.

You will find that when you are clear with your availability, it will be much easier to build in the flexibility to your working hours and ultimately set yourself up for the success of freedom which you crave.

Remember, it is okay to be different.

You do not have to work the same hours as your friends or family. You are doing something which most people will not do and that is building a business from nothing. You have to put in the work when you are working but you don't have to work all of the time.

I never want you to feel guilt for living
a different life.

Financial

When building your business, you want to make money, of

course. You need money to live, to invest in your business and to be able to do things you want.

I am not a huge advocate of only having monthly financial targets, but if that works for you, then by all means go for it. What I like to do is know what I want my business to make in the future. So although I have something to aim for, it does take the pressure off. I personally found that if I had a monthly financial goal and I didn't hit it (even if I was very close), I would be disappointed. I also found that even if I did hit the goal, I would never be satisfied. This is something I have learnt about myself along the way to building multiple businesses.

If you know where you want to be financially and the lifestyle you want to create in the long term, this can help relieve the pressure of a monthly financial goal. This way you can work towards it constantly and know you are heading in the right direction, and there is less disappointment if it doesn't happen immediately.

I think this is especially helpful with long-term financial success. You might have an ultimate 'dream' to make a million pounds in your business. I put 'dream' in quotes because it doesn't have to be a dream, it can be a reality for you. However, you might not achieve this in the first few years, or first ten years, but eventually, if you keep this as something you want to achieve, you could. Likewise, it is possible to do it in a year or two. This is why I don't like to put a timeline on success.

Another important element of setting yourself up for financial success is to know your finances. Make sure you understand your profits within your business, what your outgoings are and what you need to ensure this is covered. Remember, as you grow in business, the chances are these will change. You might have more money coming in but you will also likely have more going out. Plus, the cost of things can change so ensure you know what is happening. If you're not financially minded, like me, it can be easy to ignore but please don't!

If you need help with your finances, then please ensure you find someone qualified to support you.

When you are setting yourself up for financial success, remember to pay yourself. Depending on whether you have a limited company or are self-employed, this can be different, but as soon as you can, start paying yourself something.

There is a good feeling to paying yourself officially – even if it's only a small amount to start with. It makes you feel like your work is worth it and as the business grows, so can your payment. Ensure you know the tax and legal impacts of doing this but I believe it's important to pay yourself something. After all, you're the one putting in all the hard work!

Visibility

Creating visibility in your business is one thing which is harder to measure. Unlike financial success, which you can see in your bank account, being visible is different.

To set yourself up for success by being visible, it's about starting today. If you're not using all the marketing tools I discussed in the earlier chapter, now is the time to start. Make use of everything, be consistent and find what works for you and your business.

Ways you can measure success could be the fact that you posted something on social media to your schedule regularly for three months and are seeing growth. Or even just the fact you did what you said you would could be considered a huge success!

Networking

Going networking in real life is another way you can set your business up for success. I especially think this can be helpful for service businesses, but any business can benefit from networking.

Here are my top 10 tips for effective networking:

1. **Start with a clear purpose:** Before you attend a networking event or reach out to someone, decide why you want to connect with them and what you hope to achieve.

2. **Build relationships, not just connections:** Networking is about building relationships which can lead to mutually beneficial opportunities in the future.

3. **Listen actively:** Be an active listener and show real interest in what others have to say.

4. **Be authentic:** People can tell when you're not being genuine, so be yourself and let your personality shine through.

5. **Show gratitude:** Always express your gratitude to those who help you, and follow up with a thank-you email or message.

6. **Attend industry events:** Attend events relevant to your industry or interests to meet like-minded individuals and build your network.

7. **Join professional organisations:** These can provide valuable networking opportunities and access to industry-specific resources.

8. **Use social media:** Use social media platforms to connect with professionals in your field and stay up to date on industry news.

9. **Offer value:** Be willing to share your knowledge, resources, and expertise with others to build stronger relationships and establish yourself as an expert in your field.

10. **Follow up:** After a networking event, follow up with the individuals you connected with and continue building the relationship over time.

Public Relations

Public Relations (PR) is another great way to share your business. PR is not just about getting your name in the newspapers or appearing on TV; it's about building a strong and favourable public image for your business.

Effective PR showcases your expertise, achievements, and the unique selling points of your business. A big benefit is that strong PR strategy can position you as a leader in your field.

PR amplifies your voice. One of the challenges that women in business face is that of visibility. PR can magnify your message, helping it to reach places and people that otherwise might be inaccessible. Through media coverage, speaking opportunities, or community engagement, PR provides a platform for you to share your story, express your business values, and articulate your vision for the future.

PR also aids in credibility building. People do business with those they know, like, and trust. By consistently presenting your business in a professional and authentic manner, PR helps you gain the trust of your customers. Coverage in reputable media outlets can bolster your credibility.

Getting started with PR doesn't have to be daunting or expensive.

Here are some initial steps you can take with your PR:

✓ **Craft Your Story:** Before reaching out to journalists or considering PR campaigns, understand what your unique story is. What problem is your business solving? How are you different from your competitors? Your story will be the backbone of all your PR efforts.

✓ **Identify Your Audience:** Knowing who you want to reach will guide your PR strategy. Are you targeting other businesses, young women, or perhaps mums who are re-entering the workforce? Your target audience will influence the platforms you choose, the language you use, and even the timing of your PR efforts.

✓ **Press Kit:** Create a basic press kit comprising a company profile, your own bio, high-resolution images, and any press releases or articles already written about your company. This will be handy when reaching out to the media.

✓ **Start Small:** You don't need to aim for the cover of a major business magazine right off the bat. Local newspapers, blogs, and industry-specific publications are great places to start.

✓ **Hire a PR Professional:** If your budget allows, consider hiring a PR expert or agency that understand your business. They can navigate the media landscape much more efficiently and can often secure high-profile opportunities more easily.

Awards

Applying for business awards is another thing to consider for your business. The benefits of participating in awards go far beyond the potential of winning a shiny trophy!

Just being shortlisted for an award can massively boost your brand's credibility. Awards are often judged by experts in the industry, so receiving recognition implies that your business has passed the rigorous scrutiny of those who know best.

Awards provide excellent PR opportunities. Merely being nominated can warrant a press release, a blog post, or social media announcements. If you win, that's a news story waiting to happen.

Applying for business awards can offer you a lot more than a moment in the spotlight. Although it's an investment of time and effort, the rewards, especially if you win, can elevate your business to new heights.

Sense of Achievement

Ultimately, celebrating your achievements is a great way to set yourself up for success, regardless of how big or small they may appear. Remember that you are building a business that not many people will understand, so celebrate every win you achieve.

I recommend celebrating every achievement – no matter how seemingly insignificant – in a way that suits you. One of my most cherished memories is when I received a notification on my phone that my new product business had made its first sale whilst I was enjoying a meal. I had already ordered a glass of wine, so I was able to toast to the occasion. I continued to celebrate for several hours afterwards, basking in the joy of what felt like such a significant accomplishment.

It's easy in business to achieve something you have been working towards and then move on to the next thing without taking the time to appreciate what you've accomplished. So, don't be too tough on yourself and take time to soak in how far you've come. Sometimes, I'll celebrate just getting through the week!

Remember that you deserve every piece of success, no matter how big or small. If it's a success to you, then it's a big deal, and you did it. So, remind yourself that you achieved that and celebrate accordingly. Don't save the best stuff for the 'bigger' achievements, celebrate everything in a way that makes you happy.

N N N

What to focus on:

✗ Flexibility in Defining Success: Understand that your definition of success may change as your business and personal circumstances alter. Adapt your goals and priorities accordingly.

✗ Networking for Success: Build relationships, listen actively, and be authentic in your networking efforts. Attend industry events and join professional organisations to expand your circle.

✗ Effective Use of Public Relations: Develop a strong PR strategy to build a favourable public image, showcase your expertise, and gain credibility. Start small with local media and grow your presence over time.

✗ Participating in Awards: Consider applying for business awards for brand credibility and PR opportunities. Even being shortlisted can boost your brand's image.

✗ Celebrating Achievements: Make it a practice to celebrate your successes in ways that are meaningful to you. Acknowledge every win, no matter the size, and remind yourself of your worthiness and achievements.

"If you don't like the road you're walking, start paving another one."

Dolly Parton

CHAPTER 9
MINDSET

You are working on growing and building your very own business. You know what you want to do, what you want to achieve and all the successes you want to celebrate. The next stage is all about longevity. It's about keeping going past that initial excitement and working consistently. Now you need to keep going.

Keeping going can be often the biggest challenge once the excitement fades, but it doesn't have to be.

There will be times when your mind will tell you to stop. You might question if you can achieve the successes you want. You might ask yourself if you are someone who can even run their own business. Your mind is so powerful and it is always wanting to keep you safe in life. It's thanks to this protection that fear and doubts can start to creep in. The key is to get on top of your thoughts and change them as soon as you can.

Mindset is so important in building the successful business which you deserve. It's about to believing in yourself, even if it feels like nobody else does. More importantly, it's about continuing to believe in yourself, even on the days when you don't feel like it.

Having strong foundations and techniques which help your mindset can be crucial in keeping going. This mindset is not about being positive constantly – you are human with emotions and feelings. It's not about always only seeing the good even when things are falling apart around you. It is about recognising what has happened and switching your mind to tell yourself that you can do whatever you want. To believe that you are worthy of success and that business success is coming to you.

Another top tip to keep a healthy mindset is to not get involved in too much negativity. Discussions about the state of the economy, hearing about a business which hasn't succeeded or general negativity are all things to get away from.

I don't mean to be fake with your positivity, but don't engage in these types of conversations or spend hours reading about them in the news. Do your best to focus on protecting your mind, keeping your focus and achieving the success you deserve.

I have six key techniques which help me with my mindset and I am going to share them here. Of course, there are more actions that you can do, but I have discovered that these six are specific to helping your mind believe in your success.

All of these methods work with your subconscious brain, the

part of your brain at the back which is thinking all day long without you even noticing! The subconscious mind is the part of your brain that you want to get your new beliefs about yourself to as it runs you mind without you even realising.

You often won't realise what your subconscious thoughts are but they will materialise within your business.

My 6 key methods to improve your mindset are:

Affirmations

EFT

Meditations

Scripting

Visualising

Hypnotherapy

Affirmations

Affirmations are powerful sentences to help you change your subconscious thoughts. These thoughts can be deeply ingrained and you may not even realise you have them. When I first discovered affirmations many years ago, I had a long list of them. I would read them occasionally but eventually felt like they weren't working for me. However, when I revisited affirmations years later and said them with more intention and purpose, they changed my life in ways I couldn't have imagined.

It's important to remember that you are constantly thinking all day long and affirmations help to change your dominant thoughts over time. When you change your dominant thoughts, you change your world. If your subconscious mind is constantly telling you that you can't achieve the success you want, then there's a high probability that you will never achieve it. But, when you start telling yourself new thoughts and beliefs through affirmations, they will eventually come true in your life. So, be intentional with your affirmations and make sure they match with the success and life you want to create for yourself.

Here are some of my favourite affirmations for business:

My business is booming.

It is so easy for me to make money.

EVERYTHING I TOUCH TURNS TO GOLD.

I AM A SUCCESSFUL BUSINESS OWNER.

I am always worthy of business success.

Everything I do makes money.

Everyone loves me and my business.

When it comes to affirmations, less is often more. The key is to choose a few powerful statements and repeat them frequently throughout the day, especially in the morning and at night. Writing them down and memorising them can help you to integrate them more deeply into your subconscious mind. Over time, they will become your dominant way of thinking.

To find the most effective affirmations for you, start by writing down all the thoughts and feelings you have about yourself and your business right now, including any negative ones. Then, reframe those negative statements into positive affirmations. Focus on affirmations that feel authentic to you and that resonate with your goals and values. Remember, the purpose of affirmations is to change your dominant thoughts and beliefs, so choose statements that help you build confidence, optimism, and resilience.

Here are some examples of changing negative thoughts into affirmations:

I don't know how to make money –> It is so easy for me to make money

Nobody cares about my business –> My business is loved by everyone

I am not successful –> I am always successful in everything I do

One common misconception about affirmations is that you have to already believe them for them to work. However, it's important to recognise that you may not believe your affirmations right away, especially if they contradict beliefs you've held for a long time. The key is to keep repeating them regularly, regardless of whether you believe them or not. Eventually, with enough repetition, they will become part of your belief system. You can say your affirmations out loud or in your head, whichever works best for you.

EFT Tapping

EFT stands for Emotional Freedom Technique, and is also known as Tapping. It involves tapping on certain points of the body (also called meridian points) while saying statements or affirmations. It's like acupuncture but without needles! Tapping can be an effective way to release stress and anxiety, as well as to let go of old thought patterns and beliefs that no longer serve you.

I personally find tapping to be a useful tool for bringing in new, positive beliefs about myself and my abilities. It's a simple practice that can be done almost anywhere, and the results can be profound. Give it a try and see how it works for you!

Here are the main tapping points:

Karate Chop – Side of hand

Top of Head

Eyebrow

Side of the Eye

Under the Eye

Under the Nose

Chin

Collarbone

Under the Arm

Wrists

The sequence of tapping is important and follows a specific pattern. While tapping on these points, you say your old negative beliefs, thoughts or emotions that you want to release. Then, you bring in new positive affirmations, thoughts or beliefs that you want to adopt.

By tapping on these points and repeating these statements, you can release energy blockages and restore the natural flow of energy in your body. EFT can be effective in reducing stress, anxiety, and negative emotions. Some people also use EFT to help with physical pain or discomfort.

EFT can be used as a complementary tool to support your overall well-being.

I have created an exclusive tapping for readers of Self Wise, which you can download here: https://carolinetowers.co.uk/self-wise-eft

I also enjoy doing a shorter tapping sequence which focuses on the eyebrow, side of the eye, chin, collarbone, and holding the wrist while breathing in and out. I do this sequence specifically with my affirmations to help them become more deeply ingrained in my beliefs. Instead of using a long sequence like the one above, I choose one affirmation and repeat it on each point. This helps to strengthen the connection between the affirmation and the tapping, making it even more powerful for bringing about positive change.

Visualisation

Visualising the success that you want to achieve for your business is a powerful way to put these thoughts into your subconscious mind. Your subconscious doesn't differentiate between what's real or not, so the more you visualise your success, the more your brain will work to make it happen.

You can visualise with your eyes open or closed and imagine a scene in which you have achieved something you want. Focus on visualising the scene from the first-person perspective so that you see your hands and body instead of watching yourself doing something from a third-person perspective.

For instance, if you want to have a certain amount of money in the bank, imagine a short scene where you pick up your phone, open your banking app, and see the number you want displayed on your screen.

The scenes you visualise only need to be a few seconds long, and you can repeat them as often as you like to help your mind and body feel like they have already happened.

Select 3-5 scenes that represent success for you and use them as your visualisations for your business. Doing so will help you manifest your desires into reality and make it feel amazing when you achieve them!

These scenes that represent success for you can be anything you want. A few ideas to get you started are:

Having your first sale.

Securing a huge client.

Seeing a large sum of money in the bank.

Enjoying a dream holiday with your family.

Speaking about your success at a large conference.

You can visualise at any time of the day but a perfect time to do this is when you are in bed and ready to fall asleep.

Scripting

Scripting is the process of writing down your thoughts. Unlike journaling, which is often about the past or your current feelings, scripting is about envisioning the future. It involves writing down your dream day in your business and letting your imagination run wild.

When scripting, don't hold back. Write down everything you want to achieve, no matter how big or small it may seem. Visualise yourself as already having achieved your goals and write about how it feels. The more detail you can add to your script, the better.

You can script in the morning as a way to set intentions for the day ahead or at night as a way to reflect on your day and set intentions for the next day. You can also script for specific goals or events, like a product launch or meeting with a potential client.

Remember that scripting is a way to tap into your imagination and create a positive mindset. It's not about putting pressure on yourself to achieve certain goals or outcomes. Enjoy the process and have fun with it!

Here are some ways you can script:

Dear Diary style.

A thank you letter from a customer or client.

You dream day in business.

Rewrite your day the way you would have liked it to have happened.

Freestyle things you would love to happen.

Write down some of your affirmations.

Grab a pen and paper and start scripting! There's something magical about writing down your thoughts and dreams. It's the connection from your mind to the paper that makes it a powerful way to manifest your desires. Allow yourself to be creative and go wild with your imagination. Don't be afraid of what you write, even if it seems impossible or unrealistic. Let yourself dream big and believe that it will come true.

As you write, focus on the feelings and emotions that you would experience if your dreams were to come true. Use descriptive language to bring your vision to life. Be specific about what you want to achieve and how you want to feel. Writing in the present tense as if you have already achieved your goals can also be helpful in making them feel more real.

Scripting can be done daily, weekly or whenever you feel inspired to do so. The more you do it, the more you focus your mind on believing it will happen.

Meditation

Meditation can be an effective way to clear your mind and visualise the success you want in your business. While many people use meditation to clear their minds, it can be challenging for some. For me, meditation works best when I visualise a scene.

To meditate effectively, find a quiet place and put on some of your favourite relaxing music. Get comfortable and close your eyes. Take a few seconds to breathe in and out, allowing your mind and body to relax.

Once you have done this, start visualising a positive and successful scene. For example, you could imagine yourself traveling to the airport, boarding a first-class flight, arriving at a tropical destination, and exploring your hotel. This scene could represent achieving a certain level of income or gaining more freedom in your business.

The scene you decide to visualise can be anything that makes you feel good. The idea is to feed your mind with successful images and help you believe that you can achieve the success you desire. Remember, meditation is a practice, so keep at it even if it feels challenging at first. Over time, you will find it easier to relax and visualise your success.

Hypnosis

Hypnosis can be a powerful tool for overcoming limiting beliefs and self-sabotage that may be holding you back from achieving success in your business. It can also help you to tap into your creativity and intuition, allowing you to come up with new ideas and solutions to challenges you may face.

During a hypnosis session, you will typically be guided into a relaxed state and then given positive suggestions or affirmations to help reprogramme your subconscious mind. These suggestions can be tailored to your specific goals and desires, making hypnosis a highly personalised approach to achieving success.

It's important to note that hypnosis is not a magic bullet and it may require multiple sessions to see significant results. However, many people report feeling more empowered, confident, and focused after incorporating hypnosis into their success mindset routine.

⚡ ⚡ ⚡

Having a positive and empowering mindset can truly make a difference in your business and life. It is essential to cultivate a strong self-belief and a can-do attitude. These methods of EFT, visualisation, scripting, meditation and hypnosis can all help you achieve a positive mindset and overcome any limiting beliefs that might be holding you back.

Remember that everyone is different, so it's essential to experiment and find what works best for you. You might find that you prefer to use some of these techniques more than others or that you need to modify them to fit your individual needs.

With practice, you can learn to reprogram your subconscious mind and create new, empowering beliefs that will help you achieve success in your business and beyond. Always remember that you have the power to create the life and business you desire through your mindset and beliefs. Keep working on your mindset, and your business will thrive!

⚡ ⚡ ⚡

What to focus on:

✗ Importance of Mindset: Mindset is important in sustaining business growth and navigating challenges. Recognise that doubts and fears are natural but can be overcome with a change of mindset.

✗ Power of the Subconscious: Understand that the subconscious mind plays a significant role in shaping your beliefs and attitudes towards success. Engage with techniques that influence the subconscious for a more positive outlook.

✗ Experiment and Customise: Understand that different methods work for different people. Experiment with various techniques to find what best suits your personality and business needs.

✗ Continuous Practice: Maintaining your mindset is an ongoing effort. Regularly practise your chosen methods to reinforce positive thinking and beliefs.

"It is not easy to find a name for oneself, but it is harder to live without one."

Anne Sexton

THE END

(or is it the beginning?)

Congratulations! You have reached the end of Self Wise, and I hope you feel more knowledgeable about yourself and your business. My ultimate wish for you is to feel motivated and excited to start building the business of your dreams.

It's common to read a book like this and feel overwhelmed with all the information. But remember, the key is to implement what you have learned. You already have all the tools and resources inside you to create a successful business. There is no missing piece; it's all within you. As a reminder, use the summaries at the end of each chapter if you need a refresher on anything.

As a woman in business, you have the strength, desire, and potential to turn your dreams into reality. Your business can be whatever you want it to be. Whether it's making millions, supporting your family, traveling the world, or having a comfortable lifestyle, it's your choice.

You may choose to sell your business one day, have multiple businesses, or stick with the one you created for many years. It's your life, and you have the power to make your own choices.

If you ever find yourself struggling, revisit the Mindset chapter and focus on what you need to do to overcome the obstacle. Tapping or scripting might help, or you can find what works best for you and keep doing it.

Mostly, I want you to keep going.

There may be times when you doubt yourself, feel the world is against you, or want to give up. But those are the moments when you must dig deep, take a deep breath, and believe in yourself more than ever before.

Even if you have to start over or pivot, never stop. Never stop believing in yourself, never stop doing what you need to do, and never stop following your heart and passion.

Keep being creative, ask for help when needed, and take one step forward every day.

You can achieve whatever you want from your business.

I believe in you.

Caroline XOXO

"Someone, I tell you, in another time will remember us."

Sappho

CONNECT WITH CAROLINE

Follow her on Instagram @caroline.towers

Visit her website at carolinetowers.co.uk

Stay up to date by signing up to her regular emails at carolinetowers.co.uk/VIP

ACKNOWLEDGMENTS

Thanks to Keil, for supporting so many of my crazy ideas for so many years. A special thank you to my family and friends for their unwavering support.

I'm especially indebted to my business mentors over the years, whose guidance and wisdom have been invaluable in shaping not just this book, but my entire entrepreneurial path.

I huge thank you to my Editor and Book Mentor, Siân-Elin Flint-Feel, for her keen eye and expertise in bringing this book to life.

To the many inspiring businesswomen who shared their stories and contributed to the essence of Self Wise, thank you for your courage and wisdom.

This book is a culmination of years of learning, growth, and collaboration. It is not only a reflection of my journey but also a tribute to the collective wise words and support of everyone who has been a part of it.

Thank you to everyone who has inspired me along the way.

ABOUT THE AUTHOR

Caroline Towers is a multiple business owner and writer from Yorkshire, England.

With a passion for empowering women in business, Caroline has a goal to inspire the entrepreneurial world. Her journey as a multiple business owner has been marked by creativity and innovation.

Her debut book, Self Wise, is a reflection of her journey and expertise. It's crafted to guide and inspire women in business to follow their passions with confidence and wisdom. Caroline's dedication to her work and her ability to juggle multiple roles — entrepreneur, writer and mentor — positions her not just as a leader in her field, but as a relatable and authentic voice for women striving to make their mark in the business world.

www.ingramcontent.com/pod-product-compliance
Lightning Source LLC
Chambersburg PA
CBHW071423210326
41597CB00020B/3626